animal attacks

CROC AND GATOR ATTACKS

Patrick J. Fitzgerald

HIGH
interest
books

Children's Press
A Division of Grolier Publishing
New York / London / Hong Kong / Sydney
Danbury, Connecticut

To my wife, Wendy

Book Design: Kim M. Sonsky
Contributing Editor: Jennifer Ceaser

Photo Credits: pp. 4, 9 © Digital Vision; p. 7 © Joel Sartore/National Geographic; Society p. 11 © Medford Taylor/National Geographic Society; pp. 12-13, 17 © Raymond K. Gehman/National Geographic Society; pp. 15, 22 © National Geographic Society; p. 21 © Jeffrey J. Foxx; p. 27 © Chris Johns/National Geographic Society; p. 28 © Beverly Joubert/National Geographic Society; p. 31 © Paul A. Souders/Corbis; p. 35 © Joe McDonald/Corbis; p. 37 © Chris Johns/ National Geographic Society.

Visit Children's Press on the Internet at:
http://publishing.grolier.com

Library of Congress Cataloging-in-Publication Data

Fitzgerald, Patrick, 1966–
  Croc and gator attacks / by Patrick J. Fitzgerald.
    p. cm.–(Animal attacks)
  Includes bibliographical references (p.).
  Summary: Discusses the history of crocodile and alligator attacks on humans and the reasons for the attacks, including species endangerment, loss of habitat, and the dangers of captivity.
  ISBN 0-516-23314-9 (lib. bdg.)–ISBN 0-516-23514-1 (pbk.)
    1. Crocodile attacks–Juvenile literature. 2. Alligator attacks–Juvenile literature.
    [1. Crocodiles. 2. Alligators.] I. Title II. Series.

QL666.C925 F58 2000
597.98'1566–dc21

                                                          99-058299

contents

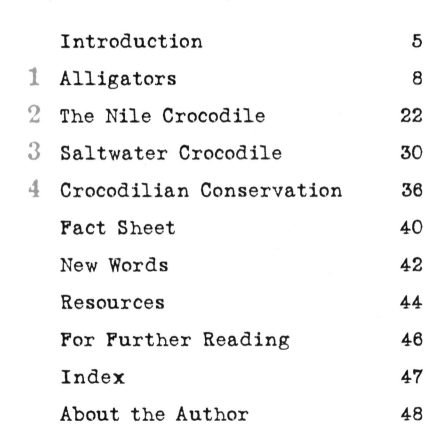

Imagine a reptile with such powerful jaws that it can grab an animal weighing more than 2,000 pounds (900 kg) and snap its neck in one crushing bite. If the bite doesn't kill, the reptile pulls its victim into deep water. Then it goes into a death roll, spinning the animal underwater until it drowns.

This incredibly strong creature is one of a group of reptiles called crocodilians. Crocodilians include alligators, crocodiles, caimans, and gavials. A crocodilian has four short legs, a long, powerful tail, and a thick, scaled hide. All crocodilians are amphibians. Amphibians live both on land and in water. Crocodilians also are carnivorous, or meat-eating, reptiles. All reptiles are cold-blooded. A cold-blooded creature has a body temperature that changes according to the climate.

Crocodilians are the closest living link to the dinosaur. They have changed little since they first appeared on Earth more than 200 million years ago. Crocodilians also were one of the world's first predators. They existed long before lions and tigers.

Because they are predators, crocodilians have the potential to attack humans. Yet only a few species of crocodilians pose a real threat to people. Man-eating crocodilians include the American alligator, the saltwater crocodile, and the Nile crocodile. The Indian gavial is known to eat human corpses that float down rivers as part of funerals. However, gavials don't attack living people.

No one knows exactly how many humans are killed by alligators and crocodiles each year. However, the number is thought to be fairly low. What scientists do know is that the number of alligator and crocodile attacks is on the rise.

The crocodile is known to attack when its habitat is
being threatened.

During the last decade, contact between people
and crocodilians has increased. This increase is
due to humans taking over the reptiles' natural
habitat. A habitat is an area where an animal naturally lives and grows. When a gator or croc feels
its habitat is being threatened, it may attack. And
when these reptiles do attack, there is little chance
of escape.

chapter one

ALLIGATORS

James Morrow will never forget the day when he came face-to-face with one of man's greatest fears. He was snorkeling in shallow water in Juniper Springs, Florida. Without warning, his head ended up in the jaws of a hungry alligator.

"I saw the head coming toward me, then I saw its mouth open," Morrow told the Associated Press. Morrow recalled the terrifying moment that an 11-foot (34-m) alligator clamped down on his skull. "The next thing I know, my head is inside the gator's mouth. He started shaking me like a rag doll. He just kept shaking me from side to side, shaking and shaking."

Morrow had been in the water for less than a minute when the alligator attacked. The gator bit down so hard that it punctured Morrow's chest. One of the man's lungs collapsed. Morrow tried to punch the alligator, but it did little good.

"My head was so far down in his mouth that I touched his taste buds," Morrow continued. "I think my [snorkeling] mask saved me. If I hadn't had it on, he could have put out one of my eyes or punctured my jugular." The alligator held him underwater for about 25 to 30 seconds. Then it released him. Friends pulled Morrow to safety. He immediately was rushed to the hospital. He still lives with the scars of the attack: teeth marks on his neck and dents on both sides of his head.

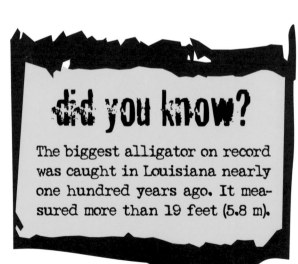

did you know?

The biggest alligator on record was caught in Louisiana nearly one hundred years ago. It measured more than 19 feet (5.8 m).

Alligators don't go out of their way

The alligator's usual prey includes fish.

to eat humans. Adult gators usually feed on fish, birds, snakes, and turtles. They also dine on small mammals, other alligators, and large prey, such as deer and cattle. Sometimes alligators will eat carrion. Carrion are animals that are already dead.

However, alligators will eat almost anything around which they can get their jaws. Their stomachs have been found to contain license plates, soda cans, and fishing lures. And every so often, an examination of a gator's stomach will turn up human body parts.

ABOUT THE ALLIGATOR

American alligators (also called Mississippi alligators) grow to a length between 7 and 14 feet (2–4.5 m). They weigh up to 1,300 pounds (585 kg). Females are smaller and usually only grow to about 9 feet (3 m). Alligators have long, muscular tails. They use their tails to swim and to defend themselves against other animals. The alligator's ears, nostrils, and eyes are on top of its head. They stick out of the water when the reptile floats along the surface. Alligators have flat, wide snouts and powerful jaws that can crush a man's bones in seconds. Their snouts contain between seventy-four and eighty cone-shaped teeth. These teeth are used to grab and hold their prey. An alligator's teeth are blunt because they are not used to cut or grind food. Instead, alligators swallow their prey whole.

HOW GATORS HUNT

Alligators are very successful hunters. This is because an alligator hunts very quietly. It swims slowly along the shore, with just its eyes and nostrils peeking above the water's surface. It looks for prey that is in its size range, such as a turtle or bird. When an alligator has located its prey, it submerges, or goes underwater. Then it explodes out of the water in one quick burst. The gator grasps its victim in its jaws and drags it underwater to drown.

Sometimes an alligator will shake its head or spin its body while holding its prey. These movements help the alligator to rip chunks of flesh from a larger animal. Because alligators don't chew, they need to tear off pieces that are small enough to swallow. Alligators also may store their catch in their mouths. The victim's body will disintegrate, or fall apart. Then, pieces of the animal can be torn off more easily. Alligators have to lift their heads out of the water to eat. Otherwise, they will drown.

WHY GATORS ATTACK

Most alligators have a natural fear of humans. They are shy creatures that usually will avoid hunting anything other than their normal prey. Yet alligators are predators and will attack when necessary. Though the numbers are low, attacks on humans do occur. In Florida, around eight to twelve people are bitten each year. Of these attacks, more than half involve children.

David Peters was attacked by an alligator while swimming in a central Florida lake.

These are the main reasons why an alligator attacks:
- It has lost its fear of humans.
- It is protecting its territory or its young.
- It goes after a dog and bites the owner instead.
- It mistakes humans, especially children, for its usual prey.
- It is hungry.
- It is being provoked.

WHERE GATORS ATTACK

Most American alligator attacks occur in Florida. This is because alligators live in every county of the state, especially in the southern regions. More than one million alligators live in the Florida Everglades. Alligators also are found in the Carolinas, Georgia, Louisiana, and Texas. They are freshwater reptiles that live in swamps, rivers, canals, lakes, and marshes where the water has no salt. Most attacks occur when people are swimming or playing in or near these bodies of water.

Increasingly, alligators are turning up in people's backyards or under cars in driveways. They've been found in swimming pools and on golf courses. They even show up on busy streets, airport runways, and in store parking lots. People in Florida register more than fourteen thousand complaints about alligators each year. Yet these same people are partly responsible for the problem. Residents and visitors often feed the alligators. Feeding the reptiles causes them to lose their fear of humans. They also

The only time it's safe to feed an alligator is if you are a professional. Here, a keeper feeds a dead chicken to an alligator at Florida's Gatorland.

begin to associate humans with food. Florida law prevents the feeding of wild alligators. Yet many people continue to put themselves and the reptiles at risk by doing so.

WHEN ATTACKS OCCUR

Alligator attacks occur most often in the evening. This is the time of day when alligators usually are feeding. Higher numbers of attacks occur during the mating season, from late March to June. Attacks also increase when it's the nesting season, in July and August. During these times, alligators are more active and aggressive.

Mating Season

Alligators don't actually hibernate (sleep during winter). However, they do slow down during the colder months. In winter, an alligator uses its snout and tail to dig a small cave, called a gator hole. Alligators will stay in their holes until the early spring. Then the longer days, stronger sunlight, and warmer temperatures lure them outside.

"That sun is their alarm clock," explains Jim Huffstodt of the Florida Game and Fresh Water Fish Commission. "When we get consistently warm days, their blood warms up. They start to move out and they start to look around. They're looking for food . . . and they're looking for mates." As alligators go on the prowl for mates, the chance of them coming into contact with a human is far more likely.

Nesting Season

Mother alligators care for their young more than do any other reptiles. As a result, they are likely to attack if they feel that their nests or their young are in danger. Hatchlings (baby alligators) can remain near the nest for two to three years. Mother alligators may defend their young for several summers. This means that there's never a good time to come between a mother alligator and her young.

During the summer months, many alligator attacks involve swimmers. To a mother alligator, a swimmer can look like a predator. The mother may attack a swimmer to protect her young against what she thinks is a threat. Warnings often are posted encouraging people not to swim in lakes, ponds, or canals where alligator mothers and babies have been sighted.

PET FOOD

Often the first choice of a hungry alligator is not a person but his or her pet dog. One reason is that a dog is about the same size as the reptile's normal prey. A second is that a dog may provoke alligators by barking and charging at them.

"That's just like ringing the dinner bell," explained Lieutenant Jeffrey B. Haynes. Haynes is a Florida official who works to control troublemaking alligators. "We had one recently that ate a couple of dogs, big dogs, 60- or 70-pound (27–32 kg) dogs."

When an alligator goes after a dog, the owner also may be injured in the attack. In 1997, an alligator killed a three-year-old boy as he was playing with his dog in a Florida lake. It is believed that the dog attracted the attention of the 11-foot (3.5 m), 450-pound (203-kg) reptile. Trying to save his pet, the boy also became a victim of the attack.

HUMAN PROVOCATION

There are many people who take chances with their lives around alligators. Some are professionals, such as alligator wrestlers. Others just want to see how close they can get to the reptiles. Serious injuries can result when people feed alligators. Teasing, harassing, or attempting to move an alligator also is extremely dangerous. There are local wildlife agencies where people are trained to handle and remove aggressive alligators.

Alligator wrestlers
put themselves at
risk to practice
their sport.

chapter two

THE NILE CROCODILE

Australian Peter Reimer was spending his vacation hiking through Zambia, a country in central Africa. It was a hot summer evening, and Reimer thought he would cool off with a swim. He undressed along the banks of the Zambezi River and began to wade in. Suddenly, Reimer felt a searing pain in his back. He was knocked into the water by the lashing tail of a crocodile. The 9-foot (2.5-m) Nile croc then locked its jaws around Reimer's right leg. The huge reptile began dragging the man into deeper water.

Reimer struggled violently with the reptile. He held onto a large rock while hitting and kicking the crocodile's head. Reimer then grabbed a stick and used it to

A Nile crocodile caught in a fisherman's net

jab at the crocodile's eyes and nostrils. The reptile finally let go. Reimer made it back to land, but his leg was almost severed at the knee. He also had deep gashes on his lower back. Investigators believed the attack occurred because Reimer had come between the crocodile and the water. Another factor was that he was swimming at dusk. Evening is when crocodile attacks are more likely to take place.

Crocodiles are bigger and more aggressive than alligators. Crocs also are far more likely to attack humans. Of the twelve crocodile species, only two are considered man-eaters. They are the Nile crocodile and the saltwater crocodile. One reason these two species of crocs are more aggressive toward humans is that they go after larger prey. Nile and saltwater crocodiles are used to catching and eating large mammals as part of their regular diets.

ABOUT THE NILE CROCODILE

In Africa, the Nile crocodile is considered the most dangerous animal known to humankind. In fact, the

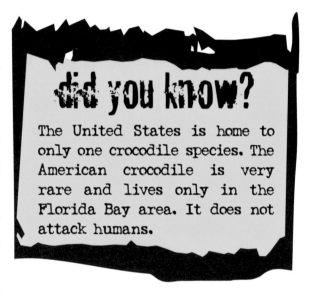

did you know?

The United States is home to only one crocodile species. The American crocodile is very rare and lives only in the Florida Bay area. It does not attack humans.

Nile crocodile kills more people and livestock than any wild animal on the continent, except for the hippopotamus. The Nile crocodile is a huge creature. It can weigh more than 1,900 pounds (850 kg) and grow to 20 feet (6 m) in length. Few animals can survive a Nile crocodile attack. The reptile is so strong that it can capture and kill a full-grown zebra in just a few seconds.

It is estimated that Nile crocodiles are involved in ten to thirty fatal attacks in Africa each year. No one knows how many people are injured by croc attacks. The reason there are so many deaths is not because the crocodile seeks out humans for food. Rather, it is because the Nile crocodile lives in almost every corner of the continent. Many Africans live, work, and play alongside these huge predatory reptiles.

One of the few studies done on Nile crocodile attacks took place in Mozambique, in southeast Africa. Researchers found that in thirty-eight of the forty-three attacks on humans, the victims were not alone at the time of the attack. Several were attacked while they were washing clothes or food in the water. Other victims were fishing, usually among a large group of noisy people. Researchers believe the splashing attracted the crocodiles. The reptiles may have thought that these people were animals wading through water, or a school of leaping fish.

WHERE THEY LIVE

Nile crocodiles live throughout Africa and on the island of Madagascar. They make their homes in freshwater swamps, lakes, and rivers. They also live in brackish waters (part saltwater, part freshwater). Nile crocodiles build dens in these waters by digging with their feet and snouts. The Nile crocodile also likes to relax at the water's edge. Here, it warms itself in the sun. Since a croc can't sweat, when the temperature rises, it will open its mouth to cool off.

Nile croc eating a monkey, one of its preferred
kinds of prey

WHAT THEY EAT

Nile crocodiles have sixty-six large teeth. They use
these teeth to catch and eat fish and reptiles. They
also eat mammals, including monkeys, buffalo,
large cats (lions and tigers), zebra, and young hip-
pos. Occasionally, crocs are scavengers and will
feed on carrion.

Nile crocodile feasting on a hyena

When a Nile crocodile attacks, it is silent, sneaky, and quick. Most victims of a crocodile attack never know what hit them, until it is too late. As a "meal" approaches, a Nile crocodile resting on a riverbank will quickly and silently slide into the water. When the victim comes within reach, the crocodile will do one of two things. Sometimes it uses its muscular tail to knock its prey into the water. Other times, it will leap from the water, grabbing its victim's head or limbs in its jaws. The crocodile often will drag its prey into deeper water. The croc then begins spinning rapidly, in a motion known as a death roll. This action drowns the croc's victim and tears it apart. Sometimes a crocodile will wedge its prey between two branches. Then it can easily tear off pieces of the body. This behavior makes the crocodile the only reptile to use tools to eat.

gator or croc?

Usually, you can tell the difference between a crocodile and an alligator by looking at their snouts. Alligators have wide, U-shaped noses. Crocodiles (except 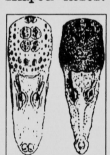 the Indian mugger species) have narrow, pointed, V-shaped noses. The differences in snout shape are because of the kind of prey they eat. Alligators' flat snouts make it easier to crush the hard shells of their favorite food, turtles and snails. The pointed snout of the crocodile helps it to catch fish. Fish make up 70 percent of a croc's diet.

chapter three

SALTWATER CROCODILE

In March, 1999, fisherman Selim Naruddin was catching shrimp in the brackish waters of the Batang Lupar River in Malaysia. Naruddin was standing on the riverbank, hauling in a net full of shrimp. Suddenly, a 10-foot (3-m) crocodile grabbed the fisherman's right hand. It quickly dragged the man into the water. His friend, Razmie Salim, watched in horror as Naruddin struggled with the huge croc. Salim ran to a nearby village to get help. When the rescue party arrived, only the victim's net and shorts were found. Naruddin's body was never recovered.

The saltwater crocodile, called the saltie, is the largest, and one of the most dangerous, crocodilians

in the world. In fact, it is the largest reptile on the planet. Male salties can measure around **22** feet (**7** m) and weigh more than **2,600** pounds (**1,200** kg).

SALTIE ATTACKS

A number of people are said to be killed by saltwater crocodiles each year, but the reports are not easy to prove. Attacks often occur in remote areas of the South Pacific. During the last twenty years in Australia, there has been an average of less than one fatal croc attack per year.

Yet terrifying stories remain. In the 1960s, it was reported that sixty-two villagers in Indonesia were attacked or killed by a single saltwater crocodile. Between **1975** and **1984**, six fatal attacks took place at the Lupar River in Sarawaque, Indonesia. More recently, nine people were killed on the small island of Siargao, in the Philippines. Officials there think that a single crocodile was responsible for all of the deaths.

Recently, Australian wildlife officials looked into twenty-seven fatal attacks. They wanted to determine whether crocodiles always eat their victims. In sixteen cases, the victims were completely or partly eaten. In eight cases, the body was moved by the crocodile and probably eaten. In three cases, the person was fatally bitten but was not eaten. Experts are not sure why crocs sometimes attack and kill, but do not eat, their victims.

WHERE THEY LIVE

Saltwater crocodiles are found throughout southeast Asia. They also are common in Australia, India, Indonesia, and the Philippines. Young salties are born in freshwater ponds and swamps in these countries. They live there until they become adults. Then they move to brackish and saltwater areas.

Saltwater crocs live in brackish river water and along coasts. Salties occasionally will travel long distances in the ocean. They have been known to swim for more than 750 miles (1,207 km). In fact, sharks have even been found in salties' stomachs!

Saltwater crocodiles occasionally show up in seaside cities and suburbs. In April 1998, a 6-foot

(2-m) croc was spotted in a storm-water drain in a suburb of Brisbane. Brisbane is a city located in Australia's Northern Territory. Earlier that year, a fifteen-year-old Brisbane girl had been attacked by a croc. It grabbed her by the legs and tried to drag her into the water. Since 1971, the saltwater crocodile population in Australia's Northern Territory has grown from fewer than five thousand to more than seventy thousand. In that twenty-seven-year period, salties have killed eight people.

WHAT THEY EAT

Saltwater crocodiles have between sixty-four and sixty-eight teeth. They eat crabs, fish, turtles, snakes, and birds. They also eat mammals, such as buffalo, pigs, and monkeys. Salties sometimes will attack and eat humans. These attacks usually occur when people have traveled into a crocodile's territory. From the saltie's point of view, a human looks just like any other mammal. When a croc attacks a person, it is doing so to provide food for itself and its young.

Saltwater crocodile eating a bird

After a saltie has killed its prey, eating can be a messy business. If the croc is not able to swallow its prey whole, it will tear the body into pieces. A croc holds the victim in its jaws just above the water's surface. Then it shakes its head and neck, tearing its prey apart. When the prey is large, the arms, legs, and sometimes even the head are ripped from the body. Then the crocodile will eat the pieces. People who have searched for crocodile victims often have found only the terrible leftovers. Parts of the body are discovered lying on the ground and sometimes even in the surrounding trees.

chapter four

CROCODILIAN CONSERVATION

The alligator population is growing in the southeastern United States. The number of crocodiles in Australia, Africa, and India also is increasing. Yet most people will never get close to a wild crocodilian. Just a few years ago, it looked as if people wouldn't be able to see alligators or crocodiles anywhere but in the zoo. Despite their size, strength, and ability to survive for hundreds of millions of years, crocodilians nearly were wiped out by humans.

By 1971, all species of crocodilians were endangered. Endangered species are in danger of

An alligator hatchling

becoming extinct, or no longer existing. Throughout the world, crocodilians were valued for their hides and meat. Alligator and crocodile hides were used for everything from boots to briefcases. Hunting, poaching (illegal killing), and smuggling of alligator and crocodile skins was common.

At that time, many people didn't understand crocodilians. They were thought of as vicious and dangerous man-eaters. For this reason, many people felt that alligators and crocodiles deserved to be killed. Also, humans began moving in larger numbers to coastal areas, such as Florida. They started building houses and roads that destroyed much of the crocodilian's natural habitat.

A BIG COMEBACK

In the past twenty years, conservationists have convinced people of the importance of saving alligators and crocodiles. Today, sixteen of the twenty-three crocodilian species have recovered from

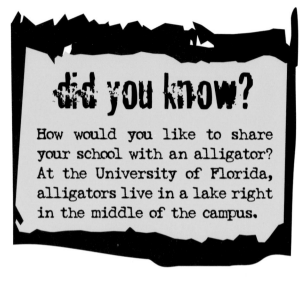

did you know?

How would you like to share your school with an alligator? At the University of Florida, alligators live in a lake right in the middle of the campus.

near-extinction. Their populations continue to grow. There are more than one million alligators living in Florida, not counting the alligators raised on farms.

Today, there are about two hundred alligator farms in the United States. These farms, which are located mostly in Florida, Louisiana, and Texas, raise alligators from egg to hatchling. Then they restore young alligators to their natural habitat. Similar farms exist for crocodiles in both Africa and Australia.

It is hoped that these farms and other conservation programs will safeguard crocodilian species for the next 200 million years.

fact sheet

Crocodylia
The scientific (Latin) name for a group of reptiles that includes alligators, caimans, crocodiles, and gavials.

Alligator mississippiensis The scientific (Latin) name for the American alligator

Life span: thirty to thirty-five years in the wild, up to fifty in captivity

Crocodylus niloticus The scientific (Latin) name for the Nile crocodile

Life span: forty-five years in the wild, up to eighty in captivity

Crocodylus porsus The scientific (Latin) name for the saltwater crocodile

Life span: fifty years in the wild, up to ninety in captivity

American alligator

Nile Crocodile

Saltwater Crocodile

new words

amphibians animals that live both on land and in water

brackish a mix of saltwater and freshwater

caiman crocodilian found in Central and South America

captivity the state of being confined or penned in

carnivorous a meat-eating animal

carrion animals that are already dead

cold-blooded animals whose body temperature change with the temperature of the environment

conservation the careful protection of animals

crocodilian a general name for an alligator, caiman, crocodile, or gavial

death roll a crocodilian's method of killing its prey by spinning and holding it underwater until it drowns

endangered in danger of being extinct

extinct no longer existing

freshwater water that has no salt

gator hole a hole dug by an alligator to live in when the weather is cold

gavial crocodilian found in India

habitat an area where an animal naturally lives and grows

hatchling any baby crocodilian

hibernate sleep during winter

Nile crocodile crocodilian found in Africa

poaching illegal killing

predator an animal that hunts and kills other animals

prey an animal that is killed and eaten for food

reptile cold-blooded animal, such as a crocodilian, snake, lizard, or turtle

saltie saltwater crocodile

scavenger an animal or bird that feeds on a dead or decaying animal

snout nose of an animal

submerge to go below the water's surface

territory an area that is occupied and defended by an animal or group of animals

resources

American Zoo and Aquarium Association
P.O. Box 79863
Baltimore, MD 21279
Web site: *www.aza.org*
Has links to local and national zoos and aquariums and tells what each organization is doing to save endangered species. Also has information about AZA programs, how you can become involved, research links, and a photo gallery.

Crocodilians: Natural History and Conservation
www.crocodilian.com
An educational resource page that covers all crocodilian topics, such as biology, conservation, and evolution. Includes a crocodilian species database, Internet resources, and pictures. You can even listen to the sounds alligators and crocodiles make!

World Wildlife Fund—United States
1250 24th Street, NW
Washington, DC 20037-1175
Web site: *www.worldwildlife.org*
Dedicated to the conservation of endangered and threatened species. Includes the latest news relating to conservation efforts and information about their programs and how to get involved. Also sponsors the Conservation Action Network, an on-line chat room where people discuss conservation issues.

for further reading

Behler, John, and Deborah Behler. *Alligator & Crocodile*. Stillwater, MN: Voyageur Press, Inc., 1998.

Levy, Charles. *Endangered Species: Crocodiles and Alligators*. New Jersey: Chartwell Books, 1991.

Perry, Phyllis J. *Crocodilians: Reminders of the Age of Dinosaurs.* Danbury, CT: Franklin Watts, Inc., 1997.

index

ABOUT THE AUTHOR

Patrick Fitzgerald is a freelance writer who has had a lifelong interest in reptiles. He lives in Brooklyn, NY, with his wife Wendy, two cats, and a dog.